The Enough Code

7 Steps To Reflect & Embrace Your True Worth

Divya Ramamurthy

INDIA • SINGAPORE • MALAYSIA

ISBN
Hardcase 979-8-89744-165-5
Paperback 979-8-89744-164-8

Disclaimer

This book is intended for informational and personal development purposes only. The author has made every effort to provide accurate, helpful, and insightful information; however, this book is not a substitute for professional advice.

This book is not intended to provide professional, legal, financial, medical, or any other form of advice. Readers are encouraged to consult with qualified professionals before making any decisions based on the content of this book.

The author disclaim any liability for direct or indirect consequences resulting from the application of any information contained within this book.

Personal growth and self-improvement are highly individualized processes, and results may vary. The experiences, examples, and strategies shared in this book are for illustrative purposes only and should not be interpreted as guarantees of success.

All examples, case studies, and anecdotes are for illustrative purposes only. Any similarities to actual persons, living or dead, or real-life events are purely coincidental unless explicitly stated.

By choosing to read this book and apply the principles in this book, you acknowledge and agree to these terms and that you are responsible for your own actions, decisions, and well-being.

Dedication

Writing ***The Enough Code*** has been a deeply personal and transformative journey for me, and I could not have completed it without the support, encouragement, and love of so many incredible people. This book is the culmination of countless conversations, reflections, and inspirations. I want to express my deepest gratitude to everyone who has been part of this journey:

To my **family,** whose unwavering love and belief in me has been a constant source of strength and foundation throughout this process. Your unconditional support reminds me of my worth on days I forget my own message. I am forever grateful to have you all by my side.

To my **friends**, thank you for your kindness, your patience and your encouragement during the many moments of self-doubt. Your belief in me keeps me going when I need it the most. I am so fortunate to have friends who uplift and inspire me.

A heartfelt thank you to **my mentors and teachers**, whose wisdom and guidance have shaped my personal and professional life in ways I cannot fully express. The lessons I've learned from each one of you have been invaluable and have been woven into every page of this book.

To every **reader who has** picked up this book: thank you for trusting me with your time, heart and energy. Writing this book for you has been an incredible privilege. I hope that these words serves you in some way, helping you discover your own worth and inner power. The real magic happens when you apply what you've read, and I believe in your ability to create the life you truly deserve. It is an honour to walk alongside you on this journey of self-discovery and self-love.

I want to acknowledge **myself**, for having the courage to begin this journey, for staying committed to the process and for believing in the impact this book could have. Writing this book has been a profound act of self-love, and I hope it inspires you to honour and celebrate yourself in the same way.

Finally, to the quiet moments of doubt and struggle that has shaped me into a more compassionate and resilient person: thank you for teaching me that I am enough, just as I am.

This book is a product of love, growth, and collective energy; and I am forever grateful to everyone who has been part of this journey. Thank you for helping me bring '*The Enough* Code' into the world. May it serve as a reminder to you, and to everyone who reads it, that we are all enough—just as we are.

With deepest gratitude and belief in your brilliance
– Divya Ramamurthy

Contents

Preface

The Enough Code was born out of a simple but profound truth: We are often our own harshest critics. In a world that constantly bombards us with standards, comparisons, and expectations, it's easy to forget the one thing that truly matters—that we are enough, exactly as we are.

For years, I struggled with self-doubt, comparison, and the relentless pursuit of "more." I looked around and saw others achieving things that I thought I needed to attain in order to be worthy. I doubted my abilities, questioned my worth, and believed that I had to change who I was in order to be accepted, loved, or successful. It was only when I began to truly embrace myself and understand my inherent worth that everything shifted.

This book is not just for you—it's for me, too. It's a reflection of my own journey toward self-acceptance, self-compassion, and inner peace. The lessons I've learned and the practices I've incorporated into my life have helped me understand that I don't need to be anyone else to be worthy of love, success, and happiness. And neither do you.

The idea for this book emerged from countless conversations with people who felt the same way I did—people who were struggling to embrace their uniqueness, people who were overwhelmed by the pressure to conform to external standards, and people who didn't believe they were enough. I knew that there had to be a way to help them, and help myself, see the truth that was always there: that we are enough, just as we are.

The Enough Code is a guide to reclaiming your worth and stepping into your full potential. It's a journey of self-love, empowerment, and acceptance. Through personal anecdotes, real-life experiences, affirmations, and actionable steps, this book will help you shift your mindset, heal old wounds, and embrace the powerful, beautiful person you already are. You don't need to change to be worthy. You are worthy simply by existing.

As you read these pages, I encourage you to reflect on your own life, your own beliefs, and your own journey. Allow yourself to embrace the idea that you are enough. Let go of the comparisons, the judgments, and the self-imposed limitations. Trust that you have everything you need inside of you to create the life you deserve.

Thank you for choosing to take this journey with me. Together, we shall explore what it means to truly love and accept ourselves, and by doing so, we will discover the profound freedom that comes from knowing that we are enough—just as we are.

Introduction: You Are Enough

In a world that constantly demands more of us—more success, more achievements, more perfection—it's easy to fall into the trap of believing we are not enough. Society places countless expectations on our shoulders, from career milestones to physical appearance, and this relentless pursuit of an ideal often makes us question our worth. But what if the truth is simpler than we've been led to believe? What if everything we need to thrive already exists within us, and the only thing standing between us and our fullest potential is the belief that we are enough, just as we are?

The Enough Code is a celebration of your intrinsic worth. This book isn't about changing who you are or becoming someone you're not. Instead, it's about remembering who you've always been—a powerful, capable, and a deserving individual - worthy of love, success, and happiness. It's about breaking free from the chains of self-doubt and embracing your unique gifts and abilities. This journey of self-empowerment is a process, and I'll be here with you every step of the way.

In this book, I will share real-life stories, personal anecdotes, and transformative experiences from individuals who have faced struggles similar to your own. They, too, doubted their worth, faced setbacks, and wrestled with feelings of inadequacy. But through persistence, self-reflection, and a commitment to growth, they learned that the secret to living a fulfilling life was rooted in the understanding that they were always enough—no matter their circumstances.

We will explore how self-compassion, the power of positive thinking, and embracing imperfections can completely shift the way you view yourself and the world around you. You'll learn practical tools and actionable steps to rewire your thoughts, let go of limiting beliefs, and foster a mindset of abundance and self-acceptance.

Along the way, you will be invited to reflect on your own experiences and rewrite the stories you tell yourself. You'll discover the power of affirmations—simple, yet profound statements that will help you reframe negative thinking patterns. By the end of this book, you will have not only a deeper understanding of your worth but also a practical action plan to carry forward into your life.

This is not a book about perfection. It's not about striving for an ideal version of yourself that doesn't exist. It's about embracing the truth that *you are enough right now*, as you are. Imperfect, messy, and wonderfully human. It's about allowing yourself to be imperfect and still feel whole.

You are worthy of love. You are worthy of success. You are worthy of every good thing life has to offer. Now, let's begin the journey of unlocking your true potential, starting with the powerful realization that *You Are Enough*!

I once met a woman, Maria, who was consumed by the pressure to be everything to everyone. She tried to live up to the expectations of her family, her friends, and even strangers on social media. She constantly questioned if she was good enough, and this self-doubt led her to make choices that drained her energy and happiness. But one day, after a particularly difficult time in her life, she had a moment of clarity. She realized that in trying to fit herself into other people's molds, she had lost touch with the person she truly was. She began to practice self-love and self-acceptance, making decisions based on her values, not on external validation. Maria transformed her life, not by becoming someone else, but by embracing who she had always been: enough.

Affirmation: *"I am enough, just as I am. I embrace my uniqueness and honour my journey."*

Action Plan

1. Take a moment to pause and reflect. Close your eyes, take a deep breath, and ask yourself: *What makes me feel worthy?*

2. Write down three things you love about yourself. These could be qualities, achievements, or anything that brings you joy when you think about yourself.
3. Share this affirmation aloud: *"I am worthy, I am enough, and I celebrate myself today."*

As you journey through this book, keep this affirmation close. Let it serve as a reminder that you do not need to change to be worthy of love, respect, or success—you are already enough.

CHAPTER 1

Embracing Who You Are

"To be yourself in a world that is constantly trying to make you something else is the greatest accomplishment."

– Ralph Waldo Emerson

The journey to realizing that you are enough begins with embracing who you truly are. It's about acknowledging and accepting yourself, flaws and all, and releasing the pressure to conform to an idealized version of who you think you should be. Society often sends messages that we need to be more, do more, or look a certain way to be worthy of love and success. But in reality, the key to living a fulfilled, authentic life is not about striving to be someone else—it's about accepting the person you already are.

Understanding Your True Self

We live in a world where comparisons are rampant, whether it's comparing ourselves to the seemingly perfect lives of others on social media or measuring our success against society's ever-changing standards. However, the most powerful thing you can do for yourself is to let go of these external comparisons and instead, take the time to connect with your true self. You are not defined by your job, you bank balance, your appearance, the car you drive, the sq. feet of the house you live in, or the number of followers you have. Your true self is made up of your values, passions, quirks, strengths, and weaknesses—those things that make you unique and irreplaceable.

One of the first steps in embracing who you are is to identify and connect with your core values. These values represent what is truly important to you and guide you in making decisions that align with your authentic self. When you live in alignment with your values, you feel more grounded, confident, and content. You stop seeking validation from others and begin to feel secure in your own skin.

Real-Life Experience

Consider the story of Jason, a young man in his late 20s who spent years trying to fit into a mold that wasn't his. He worked tirelessly in a corporate job that didn't bring him fulfilment, solely to meet societal expectations of success. He felt disconnected from his passions, his creativity, and his true self. One day, after a conversation with a mentor, Jason realized that the life he was living wasn't his own. It was a life shaped by external expectations. Through introspection and self-reflection, he began to embrace his love for photography and travel. Slowly but surely, he made decisions that were in line with his true self, even though they defied the traditional "success" path. Today, Jason runs a successful photography business, spends his days traveling, and feels more fulfilled than he ever did in his old corporate job.

The Power of Self-Acceptance

Self-acceptance is the cornerstone of embracing who you are. It's about recognizing that you are worthy of love and respect, even when you're not perfect. It's about acknowledging your imperfections and understanding that they do not define your worth. So often, we get caught up in trying to fix every flaw or live up to an idealized version of ourselves. But perfection is an illusion—what matters is learning to love yourself just as you are, flaws and all.

This doesn't mean that you shouldn't strive to grow or improve in certain areas. Growth is essential to living a fulfilling life. But self-acceptance means you don't need to wait for some future version of yourself to be worthy. You are worthy right now.

When Maria first learned to accept herself, she was astonished by the change in how she viewed her life. Maria had always been self-conscious about her body. She compared herself to other women she saw on television, in magazines, and even in her friend group. One day, she decided to stop criticizing herself and began practicing gratitude for her body. She appreciated her health, her strength, and the way her body carried her through life. This simple shift in perspective had a profound impact on her self-esteem. Maria's confidence skyrocketed, and she noticed that others began to treat her with more respect and kindness. She realized that when you accept yourself, you invite others to do the same.

The Role of Vulnerability in Self-Acceptance

A key component of embracing who you are is vulnerability. It's about allowing yourself to be seen—not just in your moments of strength, but also in your moments of weakness. Vulnerability is not a sign of weakness; it is a sign of courage. It's the willingness to show up as your true self, even when it feels uncomfortable or scary.

When we allow ourselves to be vulnerable, we invite connection with others and with ourselves. We free ourselves from the need to hide behind masks of perfection and pretence. By embracing our true selves, we not only find peace within but also create deeper, more authentic relationships with others.

Real-Life Example

Think of someone like Brene Brown, a researcher and author who has spoken extensively about vulnerability. In her famous TED talk, she shared her own struggles with feelings of inadequacy and perfectionism. By embracing vulnerability, she became more connected with herself and with others. She openly shares her own imperfections and challenges in her work, helping others to do the same. Through this, she has inspired millions to let go of the fear of being imperfect and to embrace vulnerability as a source of strength.

Affirmations for Self-Acceptance

Affirmations are a powerful tool in helping you shift your mindset and reinforce the belief that you are enough. Repeating affirmations that resonate with you will help build self-confidence and remind you that you are worthy of love and acceptance, no matter your flaws or mistakes.

Here are some affirmations you can use:

- "I accept myself fully, just as I am."
- "I am worthy of love, success, and happiness."
- "I embrace my unique qualities and celebrate my individuality."
- "I am not defined by my flaws or mistakes. I am worthy of compassion and growth."
- "I am enough, right now."

Action Plan

1. **Self-Reflection Exercise**:
   Take some time to reflect on your core values. Write them down and think about how they guide your decisions. Are there areas of your life where you're not living in alignment with your values? How can you make changes to align more fully with your true self?

2. **Embrace Imperfection**:
   Identify one thing about yourself that you have been trying to change or fix. This could be a physical feature, a personality trait, or a habit. Instead of focusing on fixing it, practice accepting it. Repeat the affirmation: *"I accept and love myself, imperfections and all."*

3. **Vulnerability Challenge**:
   Share something personal or vulnerable with a trusted friend or family member. It could be a fear, a struggle, or something that's been weighing on your heart. Allow yourself to be seen for who you truly are, without hiding behind any masks.

4. **Celebrate Your Uniqueness**:
   Write down three things that make you uniquely you. These could be talents, qualities, or experiences that set you apart. Celebrate them and know that they are integral to who you are. Reflect on how these things contribute to your worth.

As you work through this chapter and complete the action plan, you'll start to shift the way you see yourself. Embracing who you are is the first step in realizing that you are enough. You don't need to be anything else, because you are already worthy of everything you desire.

Affirmation:

"I am enough, just as I am. I embrace my uniqueness and honour my journey."

CHAPTER 2

Letting Go of Comparison Trap

"Comparison is the death of joy."

– Mark Twain

In a world dominated by social media, success stories, and curated images of perfection, it can feel impossible to escape the comparison trap. We are constantly bombarded with images of what we "should" be, do, or have. It's easy to look at someone else's life and think that they've figured it out, while we are still struggling to find our way. But here's the truth: Comparison only steals your joy and keeps you from embracing the beautiful, unique journey that is yours. The path to truly feeling *enough* lies in learning how to let go of comparison and focusing instead on your own growth and self-worth.

The Dangers of Comparison

Comparing yourself to others is a natural human tendency, but when taken to extremes, it can be incredibly damaging. At its core, comparison creates feelings of inadequacy, self-doubt, and envy. We often measure our worth against others' external achievements without fully understanding the full picture of their lives. We don't see their struggles, sacrifices, or the behind-the-scenes moments that make up their success. We only see the highlights, and then, inevitably, we start to feel like we're falling short.

The problem with comparison is that it creates a false sense of competition. You're not in a race with anyone else; your journey is uniquely yours. When you compare yourself to others, you give up your own sense of individuality, thinking that if you don't measure up to someone else's standard, you're not good enough. But the truth is, the only person you need to measure yourself against is the person you were yesterday. Growth is personal, and there's no one else you should be striving to become except for the best version of yourself.

Real-Life Experience

Take the story of Elena, a young woman who spent years comparing herself to her colleagues at work. Elena had just started her career in a competitive industry, and as she scrolled through social media, she saw her peers posting about their promotions, successful projects, and travel adventures. Elena felt behind. She questioned her worth, thinking that she wasn't successful enough or wasn't advancing as quickly as others. But one day, a mentor of hers pointed out that she was comparing her Chapter 1 to someone else's Chapter 20. This simple realization helped Elena shift her perspective. She started focusing on her own progress, rather than comparing herself to others. Over time, Elena found her own rhythm and began celebrating the small wins that contributed to her growth. Today, Elena's career has flourished, and she no longer feels the pressure to measure her worth by anyone else's standards.

The Comparison Trap in the Digital Age

Social media has made comparison more pervasive than ever. Platforms like Instagram, Facebook, and LinkedIn are filled with perfectly curated images, success stories, and highlight reels. It's easy to forget that most of what we see online is not the whole picture. Social media is a platform for presenting an idealized version of life, but it's often far from the reality of what people are truly experiencing.

The danger is that, without realizing it, we start to base our worth on these digital depictions of success. We measure our own lives by someone else's seemingly perfect moments and feel as though we are falling short. The truth is, everyone has their struggles, doubts, and setbacks—things that are not shared on online posts. The key to overcoming the comparison trap is recognizing that social media is a highlight reel, not the full story. Your worth is not determined by how many likes or followers you have, or how your life stacks up against someone else's.

Anna, a friend of mine, once admitted that she felt terrible every time she logged into Instagram. She would scroll through endless photos of beautiful vacations, couples on romantic getaways, and perfectly decorated homes. Anna felt like her life paled in comparison. But one day, she decided to try an experiment: She unfollowed accounts that made her feel inadequate and started following accounts that inspired her and aligned with her values. She also began focusing on sharing her own authentic experiences, not for validation, but as a way to celebrate her own life. Over time, Anna noticed a significant shift in her mindset. Instead of comparing herself to others, she began to appreciate the beauty and authenticity of her own journey.

Shifting from Comparison to Celebration

The key to letting go of comparison is to shift your mindset from one of competition to one of celebration. Instead of seeing someone else's success as a reflection of your shortcomings, learn to celebrate the achievements of others as a source of inspiration. When you shift your perspective, you realize that there is no limited supply of success, happiness, or love. Someone else's achievements do not take away from your own. The universe has an abundance of opportunities for everyone.

Learning to celebrate the success of others can also bring a sense of peace. Rather than feeling threatened by someone else's accomplishments, you begin to see them as proof that success is possible for anyone who works hard, is consistent and stays committed to their dreams. If someone else can do it, so can you. Their success becomes a source of motivation, not jealousy.

Real-Life Example

Samantha struggled for years with feelings of jealousy when her friends got promotions, moved into bigger homes, or travelled to exotic places. But instead of letting her jealousy take over, she started practicing gratitude. She began to appreciate her own journey, focusing on the progress she had made, the skills she had developed, and the opportunities that had come her way. Over time, she realized that there was enough room for everyone's success. She started celebrating the achievements of others, and in doing so, her own sense of peace grew.

The Power of Gratitude and Self-Compassion

One of the most effective ways to break free from comparison is through the practices of gratitude and self-compassion. When you cultivate gratitude for your own life—focusing on what you have, what you've achieved, and the blessings you already possess—you start to shift your mindset. Instead of feeling envious of others, you become grateful for your own experiences. Gratitude opens the door to contentment, and contentment is the antidote to comparison.

Self-compassion is also key. When you are kind and gentle with yourself, instead of criticizing or judging yourself for not being "enough," you learn to embrace your unique journey. You become aware that you don't need to be perfect, and that it's okay to be a work

in progress. Self-compassion fosters resilience and helps you stay grounded in your own value.

Affirmations for Letting Go of Comparison

Affirmations can help you build a mindset that is focused on growth and self-acceptance, rather than comparison. Here are some powerful affirmations you can use:

- "I celebrate my own journey and honour my progress."
- "There is no competition in life; there is only room for my growth."
- "I am unique, and my journey is my own."
- "Other people's success does not diminish my worth."
- "I choose to focus on my own path and trust that I am on the right one."

Action Plan

1. **Track Your Comparisons**:
   For one week, keep a journal where you track moments when you compare yourself to others. Write down the thoughts you have and the feelings that arise. At the end of the week, reflect on the patterns you notice. What triggers these feelings of comparison, and how can you start to reframe them?

2. **Digital Detox**:
   Take a break from social media or unfollow accounts that make you feel inadequate. Instead, fill your feed with accounts that inspire you or align with your values. Focus on using social media for inspiration, not comparison.

3. **Practice Gratitude**:
   Write down five things you're grateful for each day. Try to focus on aspects of your life that are uniquely yours. Reflect on how gratitude shifts your mindset from lack to abundance.

4. **Celebrate Others**:
   When you see someone else achieving success, instead of feeling jealous, take a moment to celebrate their accomplishment. Recognize that their success is not a reflection of your failure. Remind yourself that there is enough success, love, and happiness for everyone.

By letting go of comparison, you create space for self-acceptance, peace, and the realization that your unique journey is worthy of celebration. You don't need to measure up to anyone else. You are enough, just as you are.

Affirmation:

"I celebrate my own unique journey. I am not defined by the paths others walk."

CHAPTER 3

Rewriting Your Inner Narrative

"The way you talk to yourself determines how you experience your life."

– Louise Hay

We all have a story we tell ourselves. It's the internal dialogue that shapes how we see ourselves and the world around us. Some of these narratives empower us, while others hold us back. The story we tell ourselves has the power to shape our reality, influence our decisions, and dictate how we experience life. If your inner narrative is filled with self-doubt, negativity, and limitations, it's time to rewrite it. In this chapter, we will explore how to transform your inner narrative into a powerful force for growth, self-love, and fulfilment.

Understanding Your Inner Narrative

Your inner narrative, or self-talk, is the internal dialogue that influences how you perceive and respond to the world. It's the story you have internalized about who you are, your capabilities, and your worth. This narrative often starts in childhood, shaped by the people around you, your experiences, and societal influences. Over time, it becomes your mental blueprint, guiding your thoughts, actions, and decisions.

Unfortunately, many people's inner narratives are filled with limiting beliefs—false stories that tell us we are not good enough, not capable enough, or not worthy of success. These beliefs often stem from past experiences or negative messages we've received throughout our lives. The problem with these limiting beliefs is that they keep us stuck in a cycle of fear and self-doubt, preventing us from living up to our full potential.

Real-Life Experience

Consider the story of Raj, a man in his early 30s who had always struggled with self-worth. Growing up, Raj was often told by his parents that he needed to be perfect to succeed. He internalized the belief that only perfection was acceptable, and any failure was a reflection of his inadequacy. This belief became a major barrier in his life. Raj avoided taking risks or pursuing his true passions because he feared failure. But through therapy and self-reflection, Raj began to recognize how his perfectionist mindset was holding him back. He realized that failure was not a reflection of his worth, but an opportunity for growth. Over time, Raj worked to rewrite his inner narrative, replacing thoughts of inadequacy with beliefs of resilience and self-compassion. Today, Raj takes bold risks and embraces challenges, knowing that he is enough, even if things don't always go perfectly.

The Impact of Limiting Beliefs

Limiting beliefs are the unconscious thoughts and stories that we hold about ourselves that create barriers to success, happiness, and personal growth. These beliefs often start in childhood, from the way we were raised or messages we received from others. For example, if you were told that "money doesn't grow on trees" or "you can't be successful without a prestigious degree," or "9-5 jobs are safer, business is risky" these thoughts may have become part of your inner narrative and influenced how you perceive opportunities.

Limiting beliefs tend to show up in a variety of ways:

- **Fear of failure**: The belief that failure is a reflection of your inadequacy.
- **Imposter syndrome**: The feeling that you don't deserve success or that you're not truly qualified.
- **Negative self-image**: Believing that you are unworthy of love, success, or happiness.
- **Perfectionism**: The belief that anything less than perfect is unacceptable.

These limiting beliefs often create a self-fulfilling prophecy. For example, if you believe that you're not capable of succeeding, you might avoid taking risks or putting in the effort required to achieve your goals. As a result, you miss opportunities and reinforce the belief that you're not good enough.

Sophie, a young woman in her late 20s, struggled with self-doubt after years of being told she wasn't good enough in her career. Her boss often overlooked her contributions, and colleagues were more vocal in their achievements. Sophie internalized these experiences, and soon, she started to believe that she wasn't qualified or competent enough to succeed. She doubted her abilities, even though she had the skills and knowledge required for success. One day, after a particularly challenging work project, Sophie had an epiphany. She realized that her fears of inadequacy weren't based on reality—they were just stories she had been telling herself for years. Sophie began to shift her mindset by acknowledging her strengths and embracing the fact that she was capable. With time, she started taking on bigger challenges and celebrating her accomplishments, no longer allowing the limiting beliefs of her past to control her future.

Rewriting Your Inner Narrative

Rewriting your inner narrative involves shifting your mindset from one of limitation to one of possibility. It's about replacing negative, self-limiting thoughts with positive, empowering beliefs. This process requires self-awareness, self-compassion, and a willingness to challenge the stories you've believed for so long.

The first step in rewriting your inner narrative is to **identify** the negative beliefs that have been shaping your life. These beliefs are often deeply ingrained and may not be immediately obvious. They could show up as automatic thoughts or reactions in situations where you feel threatened or insecure. For example, you might hear yourself thinking, "I'm not good enough," "I'll never succeed," or "I don't deserve happiness."

Once you've identified these limiting beliefs, it's time to **challenge** them. Ask yourself questions like:

- *Is this belief really true?*
- *Where did this belief come from?*
- *What evidence do I have that contradicts this belief?*

For instance, if you've been telling yourself, "I'm not good enough," take a moment to reflect on times when you have succeeded or received positive feedback. Gather evidence that contradicts the belief that you're inadequate. Write it down and revisit it whenever the negative belief surfaces.

Next, you'll need to **replace** these limiting beliefs with empowering affirmations. Empowering affirmations are statements that affirm your strengths, abilities, and worth. These affirmations will help reprogram your subconscious mind and reinforce the belief that you are enough, just as you are.

Here are some examples of empowering affirmations:

- "I am capable of achieving my goals, no matter the obstacles."
- "I trust in my abilities and embrace challenges as opportunities for growth."
- "I am worthy of love, success, and happiness."
- "I am resilient, and I can overcome any challenge."
- "I choose to focus on my strengths and embrace my imperfections."

Repeating these affirmations daily will gradually shift your mindset and create a more empowering inner narrative.

The Power of Self-Compassion in Rewriting Your Narrative

As you work to rewrite your inner narrative, it's important to practice self-compassion. Self-compassion means treating yourself with kindness and understanding when you make mistakes or face challenges. Instead of criticizing yourself, offer yourself the same compassion you would offer a friend in a similar situation.

Self-compassion helps to create a supportive environment for growth. It allows you to acknowledge your mistakes without judgment, learn from them, and move forward with resilience. When you treat yourself with compassion, you're less likely to fall back into old patterns of self-criticism and limiting beliefs.

Real-Life Example

David, a successful entrepreneur, shared that one of the biggest breakthroughs in his career came when he stopped being so hard on himself. For years, he had carried the belief that he had to be perfect and that any failure was a reflection of his incompetence. After a major business setback, David realized he needed to be kinder to himself. He began practicing self-compassion and reframed his failure as a valuable lesson rather than a reflection of his worth. This shift in mindset gave David the confidence to keep going, and within a year, his business was thriving again.

Affirmations for Rewriting Your Inner Narrative

To reinforce the shift in your narrative, here are some powerful affirmations you can use:

- "I am worthy of success, love, and happiness."
- "I choose to release old stories that no longer serve me."
- "I trust myself and my ability to create the life I desire."
- "I embrace challenges as opportunities for growth."
- "I am enough, exactly as I am."

Action Plan

1. **Identify Your Limiting Beliefs**:
   Take some time to reflect on your inner narrative. What are the limiting beliefs that have been holding you back? Write them down and consider where they came from.

2. **Challenge Your Limiting Beliefs**:
   Ask yourself: *Is this belief true? What evidence do I have to the contrary?* Challenge the validity of these beliefs and look for examples in your life that contradict them.

3. **Create Empowering Affirmations**:
   Write down three empowering affirmations that resonate with you. These affirmations should focus on your strengths, abilities, and worth. Repeat them daily, especially when you catch yourself thinking negatively.

4. **Practice Self-Compassion**:
   When you make a mistake or face a challenge, treat yourself with compassion. Acknowledge the difficulty, but don't criticize yourself. Offer yourself the same kindness you would to a friend in a similar situation.

Rewriting your inner narrative is an ongoing process. It takes time, patience, and self-compassion. But with each shift, you will begin to realize that you are capable of achieving your dreams, and you are worthy of everything you desire. The story you've been telling yourself doesn't have to define your future. You have the power to create a new narrative—one that celebrates your worth and embraces your full potential.

Affirmation:

"I am the author of my own story. I choose to write a narrative of strength, love, and limitless possibilities."

CHAPTER 4

The Power of Self-Compassion

"You yourself, as much as anybody in the entire universe, deserve your love and affection."

– Buddha

In a world that often glorifies perfection, achievement, and success, it's easy to forget the importance of being kind to ourselves. Many of us are quick to offer compassion and understanding to others when they're struggling, but we struggle to extend that same kindness to ourselves. Instead, we often criticize ourselves for our mistakes, judge ourselves harshly for our imperfections, and believe that we're not enough unless we achieve a certain standard. This mindset not only causes unnecessary suffering but also prevents us from fully embracing the truth that we are, in fact, enough just as we are.

Self-compassion is the antidote to self-criticism. It is the practice of treating yourself with the same kindness, understanding, and care that you would offer to a close friend or loved one who is struggling. It's about accepting yourself with all your flaws and imperfections, and recognizing that you are deserving of love and compassion—no matter what. In this chapter, we will explore the power of self-compassion, why it's essential for your well-being, and how you can cultivate this life-changing practice in your own life.

What is Self-Compassion?

Self-compassion involves treating yourself with the same gentleness, care, and support that you would offer to a friend in distress. When we practice self-compassion, we recognize that suffering, failure, and challenges are a part of being human. Instead of being self-critical during difficult moments, we embrace our struggles with kindness, understanding, and patience.

There are three main components of self-compassion, as described by Dr.Kristin Neff, a leading researcher in the field:

1. **Self-Kindness**: This involves being gentle and understanding with yourself when you experience failure or difficulty, rather than being harsh or critical. It's about offering yourself words of encouragement and comfort, rather than self-judgment.
2. **Common Humanity**: This is the recognition that you are not alone in your struggles. Every person experiences pain, failure, and disappointment—it is a universal part of the human experience. When you acknowledge that you are not isolated in your suffering, you feel more connected to others and less ashamed of your difficulties.
3. **Mindfulness**: Mindfulness is the practice of being aware of your thoughts and emotions in the present moment without judgment. Instead of suppressing or ignoring your feelings, mindfulness encourages you to acknowledge them with acceptance and curiosity. Mindfulness helps you face your difficulties with equanimity, allowing you to respond with kindness rather than reactivity.

By integrating these three components, self-compassion enables you to face life's challenges with a sense of understanding and gentleness. It doesn't mean avoiding difficulties or pretending that everything is okay when it's not—it means accepting the full range of human experiences, both the joys and the struggles, and responding to yourself with love and care.

The Importance of Self-Compassion

Many people struggle with self-compassion because they believe that being kind to themselves will make them complacent or lazy. They fear that self-compassion will encourage them to give up or avoid working hard. However, the opposite is true. Studies have shown that self-compassion is actually linked to greater resilience, motivation, and long-term well-being.

When you practice self-compassion, you acknowledge your imperfections without allowing them to define you. This fosters a sense of inner peace and acceptance that allows you to keep moving forward, even when things get tough. When you fail or face a setback, instead of spiralling into self-criticism, you can approach the situation with a mindset of learning and growth. You are able to accept your mistakes, learn from them, and move forward with greater wisdom and self-assurance.

Self-compassion also plays a crucial role in managing stress and anxiety. When we are self-critical, we increase our stress levels, which can lead to burnout and emotional exhaustion. On the other hand, when we practice self-compassion, we reduce the impact of stress by soothing our emotions and creating a sense of safety within ourselves. Self-compassion helps to activate the parasympathetic nervous system, which is responsible for calming the body after a stressful event. This allows you to respond to challenges with more clarity, patience, and emotional balance.

Real-Life Example

Take the example of Maya, a woman in her early 40s who had been struggling with the pressure to "have it all together." Maya was a successful business owner, but she often found herself feeling overwhelmed by the demands of her work, family, and personal life. Every time she made a mistake or faced a setback, she would berate herself, thinking that she wasn't doing enough or wasn't good enough. This constant self-criticism took a toll on her mental health and left her feeling drained and disconnected from her true self.

Maya decided to seek therapy, and through her work with a compassionate counsellor, she began to understand the importance of self-compassion. She started practicing self-kindness, reminding herself that it was okay to make mistakes and that her worth wasn't dependent on being perfect. Maya began to show up for herself with love, acceptance, and patience, and over time, she noticed a profound shift in her mindset. She became more resilient, less anxious, and more aligned with her true values. Instead of pushing herself to the brink of exhaustion, she learned to set healthy boundaries and prioritize her well-being. Through self-compassion, Maya was able to create a life that was more fulfilling and joyful.

The Effects of Self-Criticism vs. Self-Compassion

While self-compassion is a powerful tool for personal growth, it's important to understand the contrast between self-compassion and self-criticism. Self-criticism is the opposite of self-compassion—it involves harshly judging yourself for your mistakes, shortcomings, or perceived failures. Self-critical thoughts are often characterized by statements such as, "I'm not good enough," "I'll never succeed," or "I don't deserve happiness." These thoughts can create a cycle of negativity, which ultimately prevents you from making progress or embracing your true potential.

Self-criticism can lead to a number of negative consequences, including:

- **Lower self-esteem**: Constantly belittling yourself erodes your self-worth and creates feelings of inadequacy.
- **Increased stress and anxiety**: Self-criticism increases the body's stress response, which can lead to feelings of anxiety, tension, and burnout.
- **Fear of failure**: When you are overly self-critical, you may develop a fear of failure that holds you back from taking risks or pursuing new opportunities.
- **Inability to learn from mistakes**: If you're focused on criticizing yourself, you're less likely to learn from your mistakes and more likely to stay stuck in negative patterns.

On the other hand, self-compassion fosters a sense of self-worth, peace, and resilience. It helps you approach challenges with a mindset of growth, knowing that you are worthy of love and support, even in moments of struggle. Instead of being paralyzed by fear or self-doubt, self-compassion encourages you to take action, learn from your experiences, and continue moving forward with confidence.

How to Cultivate Self-Compassion

The good news is that self-compassion is a skill that can be cultivated and strengthened over time. Here are some practical ways to begin incorporating self-compassion into your daily life:

1. **Practice Self-Kindness**:
   Whenever you catch yourself being self-critical, pause and ask yourself, "What would I say to a friend who is going through a similar situation?" Then, offer yourself the same comforting and encouraging words you would offer a loved one.

2. **Recognize Your Common Humanity**:
   When you experience difficulty or failure, remind yourself that you are not alone. Everyone faces challenges, and you are part of the larger human experience. Instead of isolating yourself, reach out to others for support or simply acknowledge that you are not the only one facing hardship.

3. **Practice Mindfulness**:
   Mindfulness helps you stay present with your emotions without judgment. When you feel overwhelmed or upset, practice taking a few deep breaths and observe your thoughts and feelings without labelling them as good or bad. Allow yourself to experience your emotions without trying to suppress or ignore them.

4. **Set Boundaries**:
   Self-compassion also involves taking care of your emotional and physical well-being. Set boundaries to protect your energy and prioritize self-care. This may mean saying no to things that drain you or taking time for rest and relaxation.

5. **Forgive Yourself**:
   When you make mistakes, practice self-forgiveness. Instead of beating yourself up, acknowledge that mistakes are part of the learning process. Offer yourself the grace to learn, grow, and try again.

6. **Develop a Self-Compassionate Mantra**:
   Create a mantra or affirmation that reminds you to be kind to yourself. For example, you could say, "I am doing my best, and I am worthy of love and acceptance." Repeat this mantra whenever you need a reminder to show up for yourself with compassion.

Affirmations for Self-Compassion

To help reinforce your practice of self-compassion, here are some affirmations to use daily:

- "I am worthy of love and kindness, even when I make mistakes."
- "I accept myself as I am, with all my imperfections."
- "I am doing my best, and that is enough."
- "I am compassionate with myself in times of difficulty."
- "I forgive myself and learn from my mistakes."

Action Plan

1. **Identify Self-Critical Thoughts**:
   Start by keeping a journal for one week and track the self-critical thoughts you have throughout the day. What are the patterns? What triggers these thoughts?

2. **Reframe Your Self-Critical Thoughts**:
   For each self-critical thought, practice reframing it with self-compassion. For example, if you think, "I'm not good enough," replace it with, "I am doing my best, and that is enough."

3. **Practice Self-Compassionate Touch**:
   When you are feeling down, place your hand over your heart and take a few deep breaths. This simple act of self-compassion can help soothe your nervous system and remind you to be kind to yourself.

4. **Commit to Daily Self-Compassion Practices**:
   Set aside a few minutes each day to practice self-compassion. This could involve repeating affirmations, meditating, or simply being kind to yourself when you face challenges.

Self-compassion is a powerful tool for emotional well-being and personal growth. It allows you to embrace your imperfections, treat yourself with kindness, and create a more loving and supportive relationship with yourself. When you practice self-compassion, you open the door to healing, resilience, and true self-acceptance. You are enough, just as you are, and you deserve the same love and care that you so freely give to others.

Affirmation:

"I am worthy of love, kindness, and compassion, and I choose to offer these gifts to myself every day."

CHAPTER 5

Building Confidence from Within

"Confidence comes not from always being right, but from not fearing to be wrong."

– Peter T. Mcintyre

Confidence is often perceived as something external—qualities such as appearance, accomplishments, and social approval are seen as the foundations of confidence. While these external factors can influence how confident we feel, true, lasting confidence comes from within. It is not something that can be bought, borrowed, or given by others. Confidence arises from a deep sense of self-belief, self-acceptance, and inner strength. In this chapter, we will explore how to build authentic confidence from within and why it is essential for personal growth and success.

What is True Confidence?

True confidence is not about being perfect, flawless, or immune to failure. It is the ability to trust in yourself and your abilities, knowing that you are capable of handling whatever life throws your way. Confidence is built on self-belief, resilience, and a positive self-image. It's about being comfortable with who you are, acknowledging your strengths, and accepting your flaws without judgment.

True confidence doesn't depend on external validation or comparison to others. It is independent of external achievements or opinions. Instead, it is rooted in self-acceptance—the ability to feel secure in your own worth, regardless of whether you succeed or fail, are praised or criticized, or fit into societal norms or expectations. True confidence is a deep, unwavering belief in your ability to navigate life with courage, integrity, and authenticity.

Real-Life Example

Think about an entrepreneur named Ananya, who started her own small business. In the early stages, Ananya faced countless challenges and setbacks. Many of her friends and family doubted her ability to succeed, and she even questioned herself at times. But she didn't let those external opinions dictate her confidence. Instead, she chose to believe in her vision and abilities. She trusted that she could learn, adapt, and overcome obstacles. Ananya's confidence was not based on the approval of others but on her faith in herself. Over time, her business grew, and her belief in herself strengthened even further. Ananya built confidence from within, and that inner strength propelled her to success.

The Importance of Building Confidence from Within

When we rely on external sources for validation and self-worth, we place our confidence in the hands of others. This creates a fragile sense of self-esteem that can be easily shaken. If someone criticizes us, if we don't achieve our goals, or if we don't meet society's standards, our confidence can plummet.

In contrast, when confidence is built from within, it remains steadfast, regardless of external circumstances. Building internal confidence means that you are not swayed by the opinions of others, the fear of failure, or the desire for approval. This kind of confidence allows you to take risks, try new things, and embrace challenges with a positive mindset, knowing that your worth is not tied to external outcomes.

Internal confidence also contributes to greater resilience. Life is full of challenges, and setbacks are inevitable. However, when you have confidence within yourself, you are more likely to bounce back from adversity and continue moving forward. You trust that you can handle the ups and downs of life, which gives you the courage to keep pursuing your goals, even in the face of difficulty.

The Role of Self-Awareness in Building Confidence

One of the first steps in building confidence from within is developing self-awareness. Self-awareness is the ability to recognize and understand your own thoughts, emotions, strengths, weaknesses, and desires. It is about knowing who you truly are—what drives you, what scares you, and what makes you unique.

When you are self-aware, you can identify the areas of your life where you may lack confidence and understand the root causes of your self-doubt. Are there past experiences or negative beliefs that are holding you back? Do you have a tendency to compare yourself to others? Are you focused on external validation rather than inner peace and self-acceptance?

Self-awareness allows you to challenge limiting beliefs and replace them with more empowering thoughts. By getting to know yourself deeply, you can recognize your inherent worth and begin to trust in your abilities.

Tariq, a young man in his late 20s, had always struggled with confidence, particularly in social situations. He would constantly compare himself to others, feeling inadequate whenever he was in a room with people who seemed more successful, outgoing, or accomplished. One day, Tariq decided to take a step back and reflect on his life. He realized that much of his lack of confidence stemmed from his habit of seeking validation from others. He wasn't allowing himself to feel proud of his own accomplishments because he was too focused on what others thought of him. Tariq began practicing mindfulness and journaling to increase his self-awareness. Over time, he discovered his unique strengths and talents, which allowed him to feel more confident in social interactions. Tariq learned to trust in his own worth and stopped comparing himself to others. His confidence began to grow from within, and he felt more authentic in his relationships and endeavours.

Overcoming Fear and Self-Doubt

Fear and self-doubt are two of the biggest obstacles to building confidence. Many people are afraid of failing, being judged, or making mistakes. This fear can cause them to hold back, avoid challenges, or even give up on their dreams. Self-doubt, on the other hand, often arises when we question our abilities or feel unworthy of success. Both fear and self-doubt can be paralyzing, preventing us from taking action or fully embracing our potential.

To build confidence from within, you must learn to confront your fears and challenge your self-doubt. The key is not to eliminate fear entirely but to learn how to navigate it with courage and self-assurance. Fear is a natural response to uncertainty and new experiences, but it doesn't have to control you. You can acknowledge the fear and take action anyway.

Real-Life Example

Ravi, a talented artist, had always dreamed of sharing his artwork with the world. However, he was terrified of rejection and criticism. The thought of putting his art out there made him feel vulnerable and insecure. After years of hesitation, Ravi realized that his fear of judgment was holding him back from living his dream. He decided to take small steps toward overcoming his fear. He started by sharing his work with close friends and family, gradually gaining confidence in the feedback he received. Over time, Ravi became more comfortable showcasing his art to a wider audience. While he still felt nervous, he no longer let fear control his actions. Ravi's confidence grew as he confronted his self-doubt and continued to pursue his passion.

Building Confidence through Action

Action is one of the most effective ways to build confidence from within. Confidence is not something that can be simply "thought into existence"; it must be earned through experience and action. When you take action, even in the face of uncertainty or fear, you prove to yourself that you are capable. Every time you step outside of your comfort zone and face a challenge, you build a sense of accomplishment and self-trust.

Start by setting small, achievable goals that will help you build confidence gradually. These goals should be specific, measurable, and aligned with your values and aspirations. By taking consistent action toward your goals, you will begin to accumulate evidence of your abilities, which will, in turn, strengthen your belief in yourself.

Sasha had always wanted to run a marathon but doubted her physical ability to complete such a demanding challenge. She started with small steps, first walking a few miles every day, then gradually building her endurance. As she increased her distance, her confidence grew. Eventually, Sasha ran her first marathon, and the sense of accomplishment she felt reinforced her belief in her own strength and resilience. She realized that confidence didn't come from simply wishing for success—it came from taking consistent action, even when it felt difficult.

Affirmations for Building Confidence

To reinforce your efforts to build confidence from within, here are some powerful affirmations you can practice daily:

- "I trust in my abilities and believe in my potential."
- "I am capable of handling whatever comes my way."
- "I embrace challenges as opportunities for growth and learning."
- "I am enough, just as I am."
- "I celebrate my strengths and accept my weaknesses with love."

Action Plan

1. **Practice Self-Awareness**:
   Spend time reflecting on your strengths, weaknesses, fears, and aspirations. Write in a journal about your thoughts and feelings, and identify any limiting beliefs that are holding you back from building confidence.

2. **Set Small, Achievable Goals**:
   Identify one area of your life where you would like to build confidence. Set a small, specific goal that you can work toward, and take consistent action each day. Celebrate each small victory along the way.

3. **Challenge Your Self-Doubt**:
   When you experience self-doubt, pause and challenge the negative thoughts. Ask yourself, "What evidence do I have that contradicts this thought?" Replace self-doubt with positive affirmations and a belief in your capabilities.

4. **Take Action Despite Fear**:
   Commit to taking action even when you feel afraid or uncertain. Start with small steps, and gradually increase the level of challenge. Each time you take action, you will build more confidence in yourself.

Building confidence from within is a journey that requires self-awareness, self-compassion, and consistent action. It is not about being perfect, but about trusting yourself and your ability to navigate life with authenticity, courage, and resilience. As you build confidence from within, you will find that you are not only capable of achieving your goals, but you are also worthy of the love, success, and happiness that life has to offer.

Affirmation:

"I am strong, capable, and worthy of success. I trust in myself to overcome any obstacle that comes my way."

CHAPTER 6

Overcoming Fear and Doubt

"Do one thing every day that scares you."

– Eleanor Roosevelt

Fear and doubt are among the most powerful forces that can hold us back from reaching our full potential. They often creep into our thoughts when we're faced with uncertainty, new opportunities, or challenges. Fear can paralyze us, and self-doubt can undermine our self-belief, causing us to question our abilities and worth. These emotions, though natural and common, can keep us stuck in a cycle of inaction, regret, and missed opportunities. In this chapter, we will explore how to recognize and overcome fear and doubt so that you can move forward in your life with confidence, courage, and purpose.

Understanding Fear and Doubt

Fear is a primal emotion that serves as a protective mechanism, alerting us to danger and helping us avoid harm. In its most basic form, fear is a response to perceived threats—real or imagined. However, when fear becomes chronic or disproportionate to the situation at hand, it can hold us back from taking risks or pursuing our dreams. Fear of failure, fear of judgment, fear of rejection, or fear of the unknown can paralyze us, preventing us from moving forward and achieving our goals.

Doubt, on the other hand, is a lack of certainty or confidence in one's abilities or decisions. It often manifests as a nagging voice in the back of our minds that says, "You're not good enough," "You can't do this," or "What if you fail?" Doubt can make us second-guess ourselves, hold us back from seizing opportunities, and cause us to procrastinate. While doubt can be a natural part of the decision-making process, excessive or chronic doubt can undermine our self-esteem and prevent us from taking action.

Together, fear and doubt can create a powerful combination that paralyzes us and stops us from pursuing our passions and living our best lives. However, the good news is that fear and doubt are not insurmountable obstacles. With the right tools, mindset, and practices, you can learn to face them head-on and move through them with courage and resilience.

The Origins of Fear and Doubt

Fear and doubt are often rooted in past experiences, societal conditioning, and the stories we tell ourselves about who we are and what we are capable of. Many of our fears are learned early in life and are shaped by messages we receive from our family, culture, and society. For example, if you were raised in an environment where mistakes were punished or perfection was expected, you may develop a fear of failure or a deep-seated doubt about your abilities. Similarly, if you were taught to value external approval and success, you may fear rejection or judgment, which can fuel self-doubt.

Other times, fear and doubt arise from comparing ourselves to others. In the age of social media and constant connectivity, it's easy to get caught in the trap of comparing our achievements, appearance, and lifestyle to those of others. This comparison can magnify our insecurities and lead to feelings of inadequacy and doubt. We might start to believe that others are more successful, more talented, or more worthy of love and success than we are.

Recognizing the origins of your fears and doubts is an important first step in overcoming them. By becoming aware of where these feelings came from, you can begin to challenge the beliefs and stories that are holding you back.

The Impact of Fear and Doubt on Your Life

When fear and doubt go unchecked, they can have a significant impact on various aspects of your life:

1. **Stagnation and Procrastination**: Fear of failure or making mistakes often leads to procrastination. We might delay taking action because we're afraid of not being good enough or not succeeding. This leads to

stagnation—feeling stuck in the same place without making progress toward our goals.

2. **Missed Opportunities**: When you let fear and doubt dictate your decisions, you may shy away from opportunities that could lead to growth and success. Whether it's a new job offer, a potential relationship, or a business venture, fear can cause you to hesitate and miss out on chances for advancement.
3. **Decreased Self-Esteem**: Constant self-doubt can erode your self-esteem and belief in your abilities. If you're always questioning whether you're good enough or capable, you may start to feel unworthy of success, love, or happiness.
4. **Anxiety and Stress**: Chronic fear and doubt can contribute to increased anxiety, stress, and negative self-talk. When we're constantly consumed with fear and doubt, it can create a sense of tension in the body and mind, leading to emotional and physical exhaustion.

The good news is that you don't have to live with fear and doubt controlling your life. By understanding their origins and impact, you can take proactive steps to overcome them and reclaim your power.

Strategies for Overcoming Fear

1. **Acknowledge and Accept Your Fear**
   The first step in overcoming fear is acknowledging that it exists. Rather than suppressing or avoiding it, accept that fear is a natural and universal emotion. Everyone experiences fear at some point in their lives. Fear does not make you weak or incapable; it simply means you're human. When you accept your fear, you take away its power. Instead of letting fear control you, you allow yourself to feel it without being overwhelmed by it.

2. **Shift Your Focus from Fear to Action**
   Fear thrives in the absence of action. The more we focus on our fears, the more power they have over us. Instead of ruminating on worst-case scenarios, shift your focus to taking action, even if it's a small step. Action diminishes fear because it proves to you that you are capable of

handling whatever challenges come your way. When you take action, even in the face of fear, you gain confidence and momentum.

3. **Reframe Fear as Excitement**
   Fear and excitement are often the same emotion experienced in different ways. Both are physiological responses to anticipation and uncertainty. When you feel fear, try to reframe it as excitement. Instead of thinking, "I'm afraid of failing," try thinking, "I'm excited to see how this unfolds." This shift in perspective can help you approach situations with a sense of curiosity and adventure, rather than dread.

4. **Use Visualization to Overcome Fear**
   Visualization is a powerful tool for overcoming fear. Imagine yourself facing your fear and succeeding. Visualize yourself confidently taking action, overcoming obstacles, and achieving your desired outcome. This mental rehearsal can help rewire your brain and reduce the anxiety associated with fear.

5. **Focus on the Present Moment**
   Fear often arises from worrying about the future and what might go wrong. Practice mindfulness and focus on the present moment. When you are fully engaged in the here and now, you take away the power of future fears. Breathing exercises, meditation, or simply grounding yourself in the present moment can help you manage fear and feel more cantered.

Strategies for Overcoming Doubt

1. **Challenge Negative Beliefs**
   Self-doubt is often fuelled by negative beliefs about our abilities or worth. These beliefs may stem from past experiences or societal conditioning. To overcome doubt, challenge these beliefs by asking yourself, "Is this belief based on evidence, or is it just a thought?" Replace self-doubt with positive affirmations and empowering beliefs about yourself.

2. **Celebrate Small Wins**
   Self-doubt thrives when we focus on what we haven't achieved yet. Celebrate the small wins along the way to remind yourself of your progress. Every accomplishment, no matter how small, is evidence of your capabilities. Recognizing your successes, even the minor ones, builds confidence and reduces doubt.

3. **Surround Yourself with Supportive People**
   The people you surround yourself with can either fuel or diminish your self-doubt. Spend time with individuals who believe in you, encourage you, and uplift you. Positive, supportive relationships help to reinforce your self-worth and reduce the influence of doubt.

4. **Practice Self-Compassion**
   When you're experiencing doubt, be kind to yourself. Recognize that it's normal to have moments of uncertainty, and treat yourself with the same compassion you would offer to a friend. Self-compassion helps you overcome the fear of imperfection and allows you to embrace the journey of growth with patience and kindness.

5. **Take Incremental Risks**
   Overcoming doubt requires taking risks, but that doesn't mean you have to leap into the unknown all at once. Start by taking small, manageable risks that push you slightly outside your comfort zone. Each small risk you take will build your confidence and reduce the power of doubt.

Affirmations for Overcoming Fear and Doubt

- "I am capable of handling whatever challenges come my way."
- "Fear is a natural part of growth, and I choose to face it with courage."
- "I trust in my abilities and believe in my worth."
- "I release doubt and embrace my inner strength."
- "I am not defined by my fears or doubts; I am defined by my actions."

Action Plan

1. **Identify Your Fears**:
   Make a list of the fears that are holding you back. Are you afraid of failure, rejection, or judgment? Recognize how these fears are impacting your decisions and actions.

2. **Challenge Your Doubts**:
   Write down the doubts you have about yourself and your abilities. For each doubt, challenge it by providing evidence that contradicts the thought. Replace self-doubt with empowering affirmations.

3. **Take Action Despite Fear**:
   Choose one area of your life where fear or doubt is holding you back. Take one small action toward overcoming that fear—whether it's making a phone call, applying for a job, or speaking up in a meeting. Celebrate the courage it takes to move forward.

4. **Practice Mindfulness and Visualization**:
   Spend a few minutes each day practicing mindfulness to manage fear. Visualize yourself succeeding in situations where you typically feel doubt, and notice how this shift in perspective helps you feel more confident.

Fear and doubt are natural human experiences, but they don't have to control your life. By acknowledging them, taking action despite them, and challenging the beliefs that fuel them, you can overcome these obstacles and unlock your true potential. Remember that you are stronger than your fear, more capable than your doubt, and worthy of every success you desire.

Affirmation:

"I choose to move beyond fear and doubt, trusting in my ability to achieve my goals."

CHAPTER 7

Cultivating Gratitude for Yourself

"Gratitude is not only the greatest of virtues, but the parent of all the others."

– Marcus Tullius Cicero

Gratitude is one of the most powerful and transformative emotions you can cultivate in your life. It has the ability to shift your mindset, improve your mental and emotional well-being, and even enhance your physical health. However, while we often practice gratitude by acknowledging the blessings we receive from others or the universe, one of the most overlooked forms of gratitude is the gratitude we extend to ourselves. In this chapter, we will explore the importance of cultivating gratitude for yourself, how to do so effectively, and how this practice can foster a deeper sense of self-worth, contentment, and joy in your life.

What Does It Mean to Cultivate Gratitude for Yourself?

Gratitude for yourself means recognizing and appreciating your own worth, efforts, and qualities, independent of external validation or approval. It's about acknowledging your strengths, celebrating your progress, and honouring the unique person that you are, without comparing yourself to others or seeking constant affirmation.

When you cultivate gratitude for yourself, you stop taking your accomplishments, growth, and potential for granted. You begin to recognize your inherent value, regardless of external successes or failures. It's about learning to appreciate the journey you've been on and the person you've become, rather than focusing solely on what you still have left to achieve.

Self-gratitude is not about being arrogant or self-centred. It's about self-awareness and self-compassion. It's an acknowledgment of the efforts you've made, the resilience you've shown, and the beauty that lies within you. Gratitude for yourself is an essential part of developing a healthy relationship with yourself and fostering a positive, growth-oriented mindset.

The Importance of Self-Gratitude

In our fast-paced world, we often place more emphasis on what we don't have, what we haven't done yet, and what we still need to achieve. We chase after external markers of success, such as promotions, awards, or material possessions, in the hope that they will bring us happiness or fulfilment. Unfortunately, this external pursuit can leave us feeling empty and unfulfilled, as we forget to appreciate the journey and the person we are in the present moment.

Self-gratitude is important because it shifts the focus inward, helping us recognize that we are enough just as we are. It teaches us to appreciate the small, everyday victories and the lessons we've learned along the way. By focusing on gratitude for ourselves, we nurture our self-worth and build resilience to face life's challenges with greater confidence and peace of mind.

Real-Life Example

Priya, a corporate professional, had always been focused on climbing the career ladder. She worked tirelessly, often sacrificing her personal time and well-being for the sake of her job. Despite achieving several career milestones, she never felt truly content. She was always focused on the next goal, the next promotion, the next big achievement. It wasn't until she began practicing self-gratitude that she realized how much she had accomplished and how far she had come. Priya started taking moments each day to reflect on her strengths, the progress she had made, and the resilience she had shown in the face of challenges. She began to appreciate her journey, which helped her feel more fulfilled and grounded in her own worth.

The Benefits of Gratitude for Yourself

1. **Increased Self-Worth**
   When you practice gratitude for yourself, you begin to see yourself as worthy of love, success, and happiness. This sense of self-worth is not contingent on others' opinions or societal standards. It is based on the recognition that you are valuable simply by being yourself. Self-gratitude helps you embrace your inherent worth and fosters a deep sense of self-respect.

2. **Improved Mental and Emotional Health**
   Gratitude has been shown to reduce feelings of anxiety, depression, and stress. By focusing on what you have accomplished and the qualities that make you unique, you shift your mindset from scarcity to abundance. Self-gratitude helps you stop focusing on what's wrong or what's missing in your life, allowing you to see the beauty in who you are and what you've already achieved. This shift can improve your overall emotional well-being and increase feelings of happiness and contentment.

3. **Enhanced Resilience**
   When you are grateful for yourself, you become more resilient in the face of adversity. Life's challenges are inevitable, but self-gratitude helps you build an inner strength that allows you to navigate difficulties with a positive, solution-oriented mindset. Recognizing your strengths and accomplishments in times of hardship helps you stay focused and motivated, even when things seem tough.

4. **Stronger Relationships**
   Gratitude for yourself can improve your relationships with others. When you value and appreciate yourself, you set healthy boundaries and cultivate relationships that are based on mutual respect and love. You are less likely to seek validation from others because you already recognize your worth. This allows for more authentic connections and a greater sense of fulfilment in your personal and professional relationships.

5. **Greater Joy and Satisfaction**
   Gratitude, in general, is a proven pathway to increased happiness. When you regularly practice self-gratitude, you create a mindset of appreciation and joy. Instead of focusing on what you lack, you become more attuned to the blessings that already exist in your life. This shift in perspective brings greater satisfaction and a sense of peace, as you learn to enjoy the present moment and celebrate your journey.

How to Cultivate Gratitude for Yourself

1. **Practice Daily Self-Reflection**
   Set aside time each day to reflect on the things you are grateful for about yourself. This can be done through journaling, meditation, or simply taking a few moments to think about your accomplishments, strengths, and qualities. Ask yourself: "What am I proud of today?" or "What strengths did I demonstrate this week?" By consistently acknowledging your efforts, you reinforce your sense of worth.

2. **Celebrate Small Wins**
   It's easy to overlook the small victories along the way. Yet, these small wins are what ultimately lead to big achievements. Take the time to celebrate each step of your journey. Did you complete a difficult task? Did you overcome a personal challenge? Did you show kindness to yourself or others? Celebrate these moments and express gratitude for your efforts. Every small win is a testament to your strength and resilience.

3. **Use Affirmations of Self-Gratitude**
   Incorporate affirmations of gratitude into your daily routine. These affirmations should be statements of appreciation for yourself and your qualities. Examples include:

   - "I am grateful for my unique talents and strengths."
   - "I appreciate the progress I've made and the lessons I've learned."

  - "I am proud of the person I am becoming."
  - "I am worthy of love, happiness, and success."

Repeating these affirmations regularly helps to rewire your brain, shifting your focus from self-criticism to self-appreciation.

1. **Practice Self-Compassion**
   Gratitude for yourself is deeply connected to self-compassion. Be kind to yourself when you make mistakes or face setbacks. Instead of criticizing yourself, offer words of encouragement and understanding. Treat yourself with the same love and care that you would extend to a close friend. Self-compassion fosters a deeper sense of gratitude by reminding you that you are deserving of kindness, even in times of struggle.

2. **Visualize Your Best Self**
   Visualization is a powerful tool to cultivate self-gratitude. Take a few minutes each day to close your eyes and imagine yourself as your best, most fulfilled version. See yourself achieving your goals, feeling confident and content, and living a life of purpose. As you visualize your best self, express gratitude for the person you are becoming. This practice helps you tap into your inner strength and fosters a deep sense of appreciation for the potential within you.

3. **Give Yourself Credit**
   Often, we give credit to others or external circumstances for our success, but we fail to acknowledge our own role in achieving our goals. Take time to give yourself credit for the hard work, effort, and perseverance you've shown. Whether it's in your career, personal growth, relationships, or health, recognize the part you've played in making progress. This act of self-acknowledgment fosters a deep sense of gratitude for your contributions to your own life.

Affirmations for Self-Gratitude

- "I am proud of who I am and all that I've accomplished."
- "I honour my strengths, my journey, and my growth."
- "I am grateful for the person I am becoming."

- "I am worthy of love, respect, and happiness."
- "I appreciate the effort and resilience I bring to each day."

Action Plan

1. **Create a Gratitude Journal for Yourself**:
   Commit to writing three things you are grateful for about yourself every day. These can be specific to the day or general qualities you appreciate about yourself. Over time, this practice will help you focus more on your positive attributes and strengths.

2. **Celebrate Your Progress**:
   Identify one small accomplishment or progress you've made in the past week. Take a moment to celebrate it, whether it's through reflection, sharing it with a loved one, or treating yourself to something special. Acknowledging even the small steps reinforces your self-gratitude.

3. **Incorporate Gratitude Affirmations**:
   Each morning or evening, recite at least five gratitude affirmations that focus on appreciating yourself. Keep a reminder of these affirmations in a place where you'll see them daily.

4. **Practice Self-Compassion**:
   Next time you make a mistake or face a setback, respond to yourself with compassion instead of criticism. Acknowledge that it's okay to not be perfect, and express gratitude for the lessons you've learned along the way.

5. **Visualize Your Best Self**:
   Spend five minutes each day visualizing your best self—someone who is confident, grateful, and at peace with who they are. During this visualization, express gratitude for the journey you've been on and the person you are becoming.

Gratitude for yourself is an ongoing practice that, over time, will deepen your relationship with yourself and transform your life. By recognizing your value, appreciating your journey, and embracing the person you are, you unlock the power of self-love, which serves as the foundation for a fulfilling and joyful life.

Affirmation:

"I am grateful for the person I am, the progress I've made, and the strength I possess."

Conclusion: Stepping Into Your Enoughness

In this journey through *The Enough Code*, we've explored the transformative power of recognizing your inherent worth, embracing your uniqueness, and cultivating a mindset of gratitude and self-love. The path to self-empowerment starts with understanding that you don't need to be anyone else or attain perfection to be worthy. You are enough right now, exactly as you are.

Throughout the chapters, we've learned how to shed the weight of comparison, rewrite the limiting stories we tell ourselves, and build the confidence necessary to step into the life we truly desire. We've discovered that self-compassion, gratitude, and a shift in mindset can heal the wounds of the past and unlock the potential within us.

Remember, self-worth isn't dependent on external validation or accomplishments—it comes from within. You are worthy of love, success, happiness, and all that you desire, simply because you exist. Embrace the person you are today, and trust that your journey is unfolding exactly as it should.

By integrating the practices and insights shared in this book into your life, you will cultivate an unshakable belief that you are enough. You will stop seeking validation from others, stop comparing yourself to anyone, and start living a life filled with purpose, joy, and fulfilment.

Every chapter of this book has led you here—to the realization that you are enough just as you are. This truth isn't dependent on achievements, perfection, or the opinions of others. It's simply a part of you, waiting to be embraced.

The journey of self-acceptance is ongoing, with moments of growth, doubt, and rediscovery. But with mindfulness, affirmations, supportive relationships, and a commitment to honouring your worth, you can keep moving forward with confidence and grace.

You are enough, and you always have been. Your worth is not defined by your achievements, failures, or what others think of you. It is inherent, unconditional, and unwavering. As you move forward, carry this truth with you, and allow it to guide you toward a life that is uniquely yours—one filled with self-acceptance, love, and the unshakable knowledge that you are enough.

You don't need to chase worthiness—it's already yours. From this moment on, live boldly, authentically, and unapologetically.

What Does Being Enough Mean?

Being enough doesn't mean you stop growing or dreaming. It means you grow from a place of self-love, not self-doubt. It means embracing your imperfections as part of what makes you uniquely human. And it means understanding that no matter where you are on your journey, you are worthy of love, joy, and fulfilment.

Being enough means:

- Letting go of the belief that your value is tied to how much you do or how perfectly you do it.
- Learning to celebrate your small victories, not just your grand achievements.
- Accepting yourself fully, even when you fall short or make mistakes.

Living the Truth of "Enough"

As you move forward, you may still hear the echoes of "not enough" in moments of doubt. That's okay. True growth doesn't mean silencing those voices forever; it means knowing how to respond to them with compassion.

When you feel inadequate, remind yourself:

- **You are allowed to feel doubt. But those feelings are not your truth.**
- **You have the strength to rewrite your narrative every day.**
- **You are deserving of love and belonging, exactly as you are.**

Living as if you're enough isn't about reaching some final destination. It's a daily practice—an intention to treat yourself with kindness and a commitment to show up authentically, even in the face of uncertainty.

The Ripple Effect of Enoughness

When you embody your enoughness, you don't just transform your life—you inspire others. Your confidence and authenticity create permission for those around you to do the same. By accepting yourself, you create a world where others feel safe to let go of their masks, too.

This journey isn't just for you. It's for the friend who doubts their worth. The child who looks up to you. The stranger who sees your light. Living fully as yourself is your greatest gift to the world.

A Final Reminder

"You yourself are your own obstacle, rise above yourself."

– Jeffrey Fry

As you close this book, I want to leave you with one simple, yet profound reminder: **You are enough.**

In a world that constantly pressures you to be more, do more, and have more, it's easy to forget this fundamental truth. But your worth is not tied to external achievements, others' opinions, or fleeting moments of success. Your worth comes from within. It is woven into the very fabric of who you are, and it is constant, unchanging, and unconditional.

Embrace the person you are today. Celebrate your progress, no matter how small it may seem. Be kind to yourself in moments of struggle, and trust that your journey is uniquely yours—filled with lessons, growth, and infinite potential. You have everything within you to live a life that is rich with joy, fulfilment, and purpose.

So, whenever doubt creeps in, whenever you feel less than, remember this: **You are enough. You always have been. You always will be.**

Carry this truth with you as you move forward, and let it guide you toward a future that reflects the incredible, capable, and deserving person you already are.

You are enough. And that's all you need to be.

Epilogue: Continuing Your Journey

As you come to the end of *The Enough Code*, remember that this isn't just the conclusion of a book—it's the beginning of a lifelong journey. Each chapter you've read, the affirmations you've adopted, and the insights you've gained are all tools you can carry with you as you continue to evolve and grow' it has been a stepping stone on the path to embracing who you are and recognizing that you are enough. But remember, growth is not a one-time event; it is a lifelong process. The work you've begun here will continue to unfold, deepen, and evolve as you move forward in your life.

And as you continue your life's path, there will be times when you will feel challenged, doubt yourself, or wonder if you are still on the right track. It's important to understand that there will be days when you'll need to return to these lessons. Life is full of ups and downs, and at times, you may find yourself facing challenges, doubts, or setbacks. But the tools, insights, and practices you've learned here are always within reach. When you need to reaffirm your worth, remind yourself of your progress, or shift your mindset, turn to these teachings. They are not just words on a page—they are living reminders that you are worthy of love, success, and happiness, regardless of your circumstances.

In those moments, come back to this book. Come back to the truth that you are enough. Come back to the practices of self-compassion, self-gratitude, and self-empowerment. They are always available to you.

Life's challenges will come, but they do not define you. They are part of the journey that helps you grow stronger, wiser, and more aligned with your authentic self. With each challenge, you'll find an opportunity to deepen your self-love, to reinforce your belief in your worth, and to grow into the person you are meant to be.

Remember, you are the author of your own story. And you have the power to rewrite it at any time. The path you've taken in this book is just one chapter in the ongoing story of your life. But it is a chapter that holds immense power—the power to remind you that you are worthy, capable, and enough.

So, as you move forward, keep these truths in mind:

- **You are enough, just as you are.**
- **You are worthy of love, happiness, and success.**
- **You have everything you need within you to create the life you desire.**

This is your journey. Your path. And no one else's.

Embrace the person you are today. Celebrate how far you've come and trust in how far you can go. You are more than enough to achieve the life you dream of. Keep believing in yourself, keep taking bold steps forward, and always remember—**you are enough.**

As you continue your journey, keep these principles close to your heart:

1. **Self-Acceptance Is Ongoing**
   Embracing who you are is not a destination; it's an ongoing practice. There will be moments when you feel uncertain, but remind yourself that you are enough just as you are. Trust that each step you take, no matter how small, is a part of your growth.

2. **Celebrate Your Progress**
   The journey to self-empowerment is not always linear. Celebrate every victory along the way, no matter how minor it seems. Each moment of self-awareness, each act of kindness toward yourself, is a reflection of the strength and resilience that you possess.

3. **Embrace Imperfection**
   You don't have to be perfect to be enough. Imperfection is part of the human experience. Embrace your flaws and quirks with love, knowing that they are what make you unique. The more you accept your imperfections, the more you will uncover the beauty and power within you.

4. **Keep Practicing Gratitude**
   Gratitude is a powerful tool that will help you stay grounded and focused on your journey. Continue to practice self-gratitude daily, acknowledging your efforts, strengths, and progress. Let gratitude be the lens through which you view your life, helping you see abundance rather than scarcity.

5. **Trust Your Inner Wisdom**
   You have everything within you to create the life you desire. Trust your intuition, your instincts, and your heart. When you align with your inner wisdom, you will find the clarity and strength to navigate any challenge that comes your way.

6. **Be Kind to Yourself**
   Above all, be gentle with yourself. There will be moments of doubt, moments of frustration, and moments when you feel less than. In those times, treat yourself with the same love, compassion, and patience that you would offer to a dear friend. Self-compassion is the foundation of lasting self-love.

As you move forward, remember that your journey is yours alone. No one else can walk it for you, and no one else has the same path. You are unique, and your potential is limitless. The lessons in this book are not meant to be a final destination but rather the fuel to propel you forward into the next chapter of your life.

You may face challenges, but with each challenge comes the opportunity for growth. You may encounter setbacks, but each setback is a chance to bounce back stronger. You may stumble, but remember: you are always enough. No matter what happens, trust that you have everything you need within you to overcome, grow, and thrive.

The journey may not always be easy, but it will always be worth it. Keep going. Keep believing in yourself. And above all, remember: **You are enough.** Always.

Now, the real journey begins. Trust yourself, go live your life, fully and unapologetically, knowing that you are more than capable. You've got this.

Affirmation for the Journey: *"I am enough, and every step I take brings me closer to the life I deserve."*

Gratitude Message

As you reach the end of this journey, I want to take a moment to express my deepest gratitude to you, the reader. Thank you for choosing to embark on this path of self-discovery, empowerment, and growth. Your decision to invest time in reading these words is an act of love toward yourself, and that is something truly beautiful.

I am deeply honoured to have been a part of your journey, even in this small way. The fact that you've opened yourself to the possibility of change and self-empowerment shows a strength and courage that deserves to be celebrated. By engaging with these pages, you have already taken an important step in embracing your inherent worth and potential.

Remember, the journey doesn't end here. Every time you choose to believe in yourself, every time you practice self-compassion, and every time you honour your uniqueness, you are showing gratitude to yourself. And that is the most powerful gift you can give.

So, thank you. Thank you for your willingness to grow, to embrace the truth that you are enough, and for your commitment to living a life filled with love, purpose, and authenticity.

May you always find reasons to be grateful for the person you are, and may you continue to move forward with confidence, knowing that you are worthy of every good thing life has to offer.

With heartfelt gratitude,
Divya Ramamurthy

Additional Resources for Continued Growth

Here are some tools to help you stay grounded in your worth, continue your inner work, and expand the practice of living from a place of "enoughness."

Daily Affirmations for Self-Worth

Use these affirmations to reinforce your belief that you are enough:

- "I am worthy of all the love, success and peace that comes my way."
- "I accept myself exactly as I am, with all my flaws and strengths."
- "I trust in my abilities and make choices from a place of strength."
- "My past does not define me. Today, I choose to honour my growth."
- "Every day, I am growing into the best version of myself."

Guided Journal Prompts for Reflection

Journaling helps you track your progress and deepen your understanding of your worth. Here are prompts to explore:

1. **Reflect on your strengths**: Write about three things you admire about yourself. These can be personality traits, actions you've taken, or accomplishments that are meaningful to you.
2. **Celebrate your growth**: Think about a time when you challenged self-doubt and overcame it. How did that make you feel?
3. **Reframe a recent negative thought**: Take a moment to explore a recent time when you felt "not enough." Write down the limiting belief and reframe it in a positive, empowering way.
4. **Release your perfectionism**: Describe an area of your life where you've been striving for perfection. Write a compassionate letter to yourself, encouraging yourself to embrace imperfection.

5. **Imagine your empowered future**: Visualize the person you want to become—one who fully embraces their enoughness. How do they behave? What choices do they make? How do they walk through life with confidence?

Self-Compassion Meditation

Self-compassion is key to embracing your enoughness. Here's a simple meditation to practice:

1. **Find a quiet space** and sit in a comfortable position. Close your eyes and take several deep breaths.
2. **Place your hands on your heart** and focus on the warmth of your touch.
3. **Silently repeat these words**: "I am enough. I am worthy of love and compassion. I release any self-judgment. I am deserving of peace and happiness, just as I am."
4. **Visualize a soft, loving light** surrounding you. Allow that light to embrace your whole being—your flaws, your pain, and your beauty—all of you.
5. **End the meditation** by placing your hands back on your lap, taking a deep breath, and silently thanking yourself for this moment of self-compassion.

Final Words

You are worthy of all the love, success, peace, and joy that life has to offer.

Throughout this book, we've explored the importance of embracing your authentic self, letting go of self-doubt, and cultivating a deep sense of self-love and gratitude. But it's crucial to remember that this journey doesn't stop here. The truth that you are enough is something that will continue to guide you every day, no matter where life leads you.

You will face challenges, moments of doubt, and times when you question your worth. But each time that happens, remind yourself of the wisdom you've gained through this book. You are not defined by your struggles, mistakes, or fears. You are defined by your strength, your resilience, and the love you have for yourself.

The power to change, to grow, and to create the life you deserve has always been inside you. The moment you decide to believe in your worth is the moment you unlock endless possibilities. Trust in yourself, in your journey, and in the truth that you are enough.

Your life is yours to create. So create it with confidence, with love, and with the knowing that you are more than enough to achieve everything you've ever dreamed of.

Take these words with you:

You are enough, just as you are. And that's all you need to be.

About the Author

Divya Ramamurthy is a dedicated self-improvement enthusiast, a passionate advocate for personal growth and transformation. With a deep interest in self-improvement, she has spent some quality time last few years by traveling, meeting people and exploring strategies for success, happiness, and fulfilment.

Inspired by her own journey of overcoming challenges and achieving breakthroughs, Divya aims to empower readers with practical insights and actionable steps to create a better life and importance of embracing your authentic self.

This book marks her debut as an author, reflecting a commitment to helping others unlock their full potential; sharing valuable strategies to inspire readers to take control of their lives, build confidence and achieve their goals. Through her writing, Divya hopes to make self-growth accessible to everyone, encouraging readers to embrace change, cultivate resilience, and create a life they truly desire.

Now, trust yourself and go live your life, fully and unapologetically; knowing that you are more than capable. You've got this!

Namastē

NOTES

www.ingramcontent.com/pod-product-compliance
Lightning Source LLC
LaVergne TN
LVHW021200160826
845679LV00024B/2189
* 9 7 9 8 8 9 7 4 4 1 6 4 8 *